THE INVESTING CODE

SACRED JEWISH WISDOM FOR THE WISE INVESTOR

H.W. CHARLES

An investment in knowledge pays the best interest.

—*BENJAMIN FRANKLIN*

CONTENTS

INTRODUCTION

Investing in assets is the key to accumulating great wealth. The majority of people work hard for their money. With wise investing, it's possible to have every dollar you earn work hard for you.

Investing wisely is one of the main reasons many Jews are financially better off than the majority of people. Early in life, many Jews invest in high-risk, high-return financial assets and accumulate wealth quickly.[1]

How does one make wise and informed decisions when investing their hard-earned money? There is a plethora of information from books, television, newspapers, and magazines. However, much of the available investment advice is speculative at best, and downright wrong at worst.

To succeed, you must follow in the footsteps of those who have a proven track record of success with investing and the management of money.

Jews are known to be the most successful and best-performing hedge-fund managers, investors, and traders in the world. Out of the best 25 money managers since the advent of

American Capitalism, 17 are Jewish! Some of those in the top 25 are very famous: George Soros, Steven Cohen, James Simon, David Tepper, John Paulson, Carl Icahn, Daniel Loeb, Leon Cooperman, Seth Klarman, Israel Englander, David Einhorn, and Bruce Kovner.

Professor of Sociology Lisa A. Keister has discovered that one of the key components of the financial and investing success of Jews is their religion—Judaism. "Religion keeps coming up in any model you run to explain wealth," says Keister, author of the study, *Religion and Wealth: The Role of Religious Affiliation and Participation in Early Adult Asset Accumulation.*

Although there are many religious texts that contain great wisdom, it is the Jewish religious texts, such as the Tanakh and the Talmud, that contain valuable information on acquiring wealth and investing it prudently.

The Tanakh (also known as the Old Testament Bible) is not some old religious guidebook that isn't relevant today. The time-tested wisdom that is secretly hidden within its pages has worked to help the Jews accumulate wealth, generation after generation. The Tanakh is composed of three parts: Torah ("Teaching"), Nevi'im ("Prophets"), and Ketuvim ("Writings").

The Tanakh can be called the greatest textbook on prosperity ever written. "Yes, keep this book of the Torah on your lips, and meditate on it day and night, so that you will take care to act according to everything written in it. Then your undertakings will prosper, and you will succeed." (Complete Jewish Bible, Joshua 1:8) Reading the Tanakh regularly, as well as applying its wise investment advice, is a practice that will benefit everyone immensely.

The richest man of all time—when wealth is measured as a percentage of the national economy—was John D. Rockefeller. He once said, "God gave me my money. I believe the power to make money is a gift from God." The Tanakh clearly states that God gives you "the power to get wealth, in order to confirm his covenant, which he swore to your ancestors, as is happening even today." (Complete Jewish Bible, Deuteronomy 8:18) "Everyone to whom God has given riches and wealth, along with the power to enjoy it...this is a gift of God." (Complete Jewish Bible, Ecclesiastes 5:19)

For non-religious readers, this book takes into account the fact that the term *God* can also refer to an invisible power or divine force that is the source of all abundance and that governs law and order in the universe, such as the Law of Gravity.

The Tanakh has many secrets contained within its text. Rabbi and Kabbalist Menasseh ben Israel said, "There is no single letter in the Scriptures whereon a thousand secrets do not hang." The Talmud can be used to decode the secret meanings and messages in the Tanakh.

The Investing Code discussed in this book is found in the Tanakh and is decoded by the Talmud and other Jewish religious texts. Decoding a secret message in the Tanakh will help you interpret the underlying meaning and learn how to apply it to your investing and business practices.

Many of the quotations from the Tanakh in this book come from the Complete Jewish Bible (CJB) and the Jewish Publication Society Bible (JPS).In the Tanakh, the term "Adonai" is another name for God. Various English translations of the Old Testament Bible will also be used.

Success in investing requires a disciplined approach and diligent planning. "The plans of the diligent lead only to abundance; but all who rush in arrive only at want." (CJB, Proverbs 21:5) This book will assist you in diligently planning and selecting your investments.

Poorly constructed investment portfolios are a global epidemic. That's why it's important to make your main investing objectives very clear before investing: Are you investing to get wealthy? Are you investing to secure a comfortable retirement? Or, are you investing for the thrill of it?

There are three types of investors mentioned in this book: The clever investor, the average investor, and the unsuccessful investor.

The clever investor is focused on investing to get wealthy. They do their research and invest for a specified period of time (one to ten years). Investing to get wealthy requires an active approach of time, effort, research, study, and a certain degree of risk.

The average investor is focused on investing to secure a comfortable retirement. They simply want to set up a solid, autopilot retirement portfolio. They use proper diversification and a set-it-and-forget-it strategy of long-term investing (30 years and up) with annual portfolio rebalancing and dividend reinvesting. This strategy liberates you from trying to forecast what the financial markets will do.

The unsuccessful investor is focused on the thrill of investing and is in a hurry to make millions within a short period of time. (Proverbs 19:2) They base their investing decisions on opinions and speculations. Fred Schwed has wisely said, "Speculation is an effort, probably unsuccessful, to turn a little money into a lot. Investment is an effort, which should be successful, to prevent a lot of money from becoming a little."

Unsuccessful investors do not diversify properly, and they place all their eggs in one basket, resulting in a high degree of risk. (Ecclesiastes 11:2) A person in a hurry to get rich is bound to make mistakes, encounter trouble (Proverbs 28:20) and, worse yet, lose all their savings on a bad investment decision. (Proverbs 28:22)

Both the clever investor and the average investor consult with several reputable investment advisors when evaluating potential investments. The Tanakh says, "For with clever strategy you wage your war, and victory comes from having many advisers. (CJB, Proverbs 24:6)

Clever investors spend the time to plan, deliberate, and consult with many advisors. They do not trust in their "own cleverness." (New International Version, Proverbs 23:4) They know that "without deliberation, plans go wrong; but with many advisers, they succeed." (CJB, Proverbs 15:22) The English Standard Version Bible says the same thing in a marginally different way: "Without counsel plans fail, but with many advisers they succeed." (Proverbs 15:22)

The unsuccessful investor is proud in their investment ability and they are not humble enough to consult with numerous investment advisors. The Tanakh says, "First comes pride, then disgrace; but with the humble is wisdom." (CJB, Proverbs 11:2)

CHAPTER ONE

CODE #1: ASSET ALLOCATION

CODE:
Bind up the money in thy hand.
Tanakh (JPS, Deuteronomy 14:25)

DECODED:
One's money should always be ready to hand. A person should always divide his money into three: one third in land, one third in commerce, and one third at hand.
Talmud (BavaMetzia 42a)

The Talmud teaches that "One's money should always be ready to hand," meaning that you should always have money ready for investments and you should divide your money properly among various asset classes.

Asset allocation is a term for describing the percentage of each asset class you should have in your portfolio. Deciding on proper asset allocation is the first and most important decision an investor needs to make because it determines an investor's future returns as well as losses incurred during a bear market.

Spreading your investment across various assets with low correlation to each other will reduce your risk and improve the overall performance of your portfolio. Asset allocation explains about 90% of the period-to-period variability of a portfolio and ultimately accounts for 100% of the absolute level of returns.[2]

Assets distinct from one another don't move up and down at the same time or at the same rate—when some assets are performing poorly, others may be performing very well.

The Tanakh instructs, "Divide a portion into seven, yea, even into eight." (JPS, Ecclesiastes 11:2) To be properly diversified, it is wise to select seven or eight asset classes and invest in them—better still, invest in ten asset classes.

Asset classes to consider investing in through index funds or ETFs include domestic stocks, international stocks, emerging market stocks, bonds, TIPS, real estate, commodities, farmland, timberland, infrastructure, and private equity.

Broad ETFs and index funds allow investors to buy the entire market in each asset class. For example, the entire stock market can be bought with a Total World Stock ETF or the entire U.S. stock market can be purchased with a Total U.S Stock Market ETF. Low-cost, broad ETFs and index funds are available through an online broker such as Vanguard (www.vanguard.com) or Betterment (www.betterment.com).

The most traditional asset classes are stocks and bonds. It's important to ensure that stock and bond allocation is correct before deciding on the percentage of other assets to own in an investment portfolio.

Hard assets that are critical to the maintenance of industrial civilization should be in everyone's investment portfolio, even if they are only a small percentage of an investment portfolio.

Asset allocation should be the major focus of an investor's strategy. Holding every major asset class will ensure adequate long-term returns.

Once each asset class is part of your portfolio, it's important to hold them even when they are performing poorly. The asset classes with the highest future returns tend to be the ones that are currently the worst-performing assets and the most unpopular.

Every year at least one or two asset classes will perform poorly. That's no reason to sell them as many people do. The most important factor is the long-term behavior of your retirement portfolio.

Determining how much to invest in each asset class is a matter of expertise and risk tolerance. However, decisions must not be based on opinions and speculations.

The average investor focused on having a comfortable retirement uses a disciplined approach to diversification, deciding on a fair percentage to invest into each asset class for the long-term (30 years and longer). For example: 25% stocks, 25% bonds, 20% TIPS, 15% REITs, 10% commodities, and 5% timberland.

The average investor sticks to a buy-and-hold strategy, holding onto many asset classes and never selling, regardless of how each asset class is performing. It's a set-it-and-forget-it strategy of investing, except for portfolio rebalancing and dividend reinvesting which you can do by yourself once a year or have a robo-advisor handle that.

Disciplined portfolio rebalancing and dividend reinvesting must be conducted annually unless you are using a robo-advisor. Most investors increase their stock allocations when prices are high. However, with annual rebalancing to fulfill the asset allocation upon which you have decided, you will be buying low and selling high automatically.

A clever investor focused on steady wealth creation will do their research and shrewdly invest in a way that maximizes their gains and minimizes their risk during a specified period of time (one to ten years). It's an active strategy of investing that is suitable for younger investors. They will invest a higher percentage in asset classes with a potential for growth over the next several years and a much lower percentage in asset classes in which they see trouble coming over the next several years. "The clever see trouble coming and hide; the simple go on and pay the penalty." (CJB, Proverbs 22:3)

The clever investor, just like the average investor, does not make asset allocation decisions based on opinions and speculations. The clever investor bases their decisions on economic studies regarding demand and supply as well as growth predictions. There are several reputable sources online that offer country and sector risk assessment.

Both the clever investor and the average investor consults with many investment advisors when deciding on an appropriate asset allocation. The Tanakh says, "For with clever strategy you wage your war, and victory comes from having many advisers." (CJB, Proverbs 24:6)

The unsuccessful investor makes investing decisions based on opinions and speculations. They do not diversify properly, placing all bets on only one or two asset classes—for example, investing only in stocks or investing only in gold and silver. The unsuccessful investor is not humble enough to consult with investment advisors. The New International Version says, "When pride comes, then comes disgrace, but with humility comes wisdom." (Proverbs 11:2)

STOCKS AND BONDS

The question of what a person should do to become rich is discussed in the Talmud; one answer is to engage in much business and deal honestly (T. Niddah 70b). The Talmud recommends investing in business. It says, "A hundred zuz in business means meat and wine every day." (Yebamoth 63a) A common method of investing in business is through purchasing stocks(equities).

Many academic studies show that stocks have the highest return on investment in the long-term, although they do carry risk.

With stock ownership, you are entitled to a portion of the company's profits. The more shares you own, the larger the portion of the company you own.

In asset allocation planning, the decision with respect to the percentage of stocks versus bonds in one's portfolio is an important one. Both are equally important to own in one's portfolio.

Bonds are considered the fixed-income portion of a portfolio. Those in high income-tax brackets can obtain a better net yield from tax-free bonds bought outside their retirement accounts.

Bonds can help lower the risk of stocks, and stocks can help increase the return potential of a portfolio over time. The industry standard for a retirement portfolio is owning 60% stocks and 40% bonds, but that allocation may not be right for you. Many financial advisers are increasingly moving away from this old and traditional model because the 60/40 allocation is not considered aggressive enough, especially for young investors.

Age is one way to decide on stock and bond allocation. For example, a 30-year-old investor would allocate 30% of his or her portfolio to bonds and the rest to stocks. An 80-year-old investor, who needs to be more conservative, would allocate 80% to bonds.

In the short-term, stocks can be volatile and risky, but in the long-term (over 30 years), they have historically been shown to produce higher returns than bonds. Therefore, they should be part of a retirement portfolio.

Financial experts recommended keeping bond maturities short—preferably less than five years. Therefore, it is advisable to only hold short-term bonds in your retirement portfolio, including Treasury Bills (T-bills) and notes, short-term corporate, government agency, and municipal bonds. Long-duration bonds are generally volatile, are vulnerable to the ravages of inflation, and have low long-term returns.

Treasury Inflation Protected Securities (TIPS) are inflation-protected bonds. The principal of a TIPS increases with inflation and decreases with deflation. TIPS should be included in a portfolio's fixed income allocation.

During severe bear markets, many investors flee stocks and equity mutual funds. However, by abandoning the stock market during steep downturns, investors miss out on subsequent recoveries.

Many investors know the adage "buy low and sell high," but only clever investors are capable of doing so—buying stocks when they are at their lowest during bear market recoveries and when the Fear and Greed Index declares that investor sentiment is "fear."

The Intelligent Investor (2006) by Benjamin Graham says, "The market is a pendulum that forever swings between unsustainable optimism (which makes stocks to expensive and unjustified pessimism (which makes them too cheap)."

The clever investor realizes that stocks become riskier, not less, as their prices increase. Benjamin Graham said, "A great company is not a great investment if you pay too much for the stock."

Clever investors dread a bull market because it makes stocks more expensive to buy and they gladly welcome a bear market because it puts stocks back on sale.

Ideally, an investor should buy and hold stocks when they are cheap, and sell them when they become overpriced and keep their funds in bonds and cash until stocks become cheap enough to buy again.

Falling stock prices are great news for any investor with a very long time horizon because they enable the investor to buy more stocks for less money.

Warren Buffett, considered to be the most successful investor in the world, said, "Be fearful when others are greedy and greedy when others are fearful." It's hard for many investors to put this wise advice into practice, as most people follow the crowd's sentiments and emotions regarding the stock market. It requires a contrarian attitude to invest for the purposes of wealth creation.

INTERNATIONAL STOCKS

A primary reason to increase the asset allocation in your investment portfolio for international stocks and emerging markets is diversification.

Diversification reduces risk because investing in markets that are not perfectly correlated provides the potential for gains in one part of your portfolio to offset poor performance in another.

A truly diversified portfolio is global and contains a fair percentage of international markets and emerging markets .Many financial advisors suggest that between 35% and 50% of a portfolio's stock holdings should be in international stocks.

An internationally diversified portfolio is likely to have higher returns with significantly less risk, as it is more diversified than a portfolio invested in only one country's stock market.

A clever investor will study the global stock markets as well as stock market valuations and allocate a part of their total investment portfolio to undervalued international markets positioned for growth rather than expensive and overvalued markets where the investor sentiment is greed.

An average investor will review their current investments and ask themselves whether their portfolio is global enough. If not, they will add an international stock ETF or index fund to their portfolio. In his book, *Financial Fitness Forever,* investing expert Paul A. Merriman recommends putting half of stock allocation to international stocks.

Vanguard Total International Stock ETF (VXUS) offers exposure to both international developed markets as well as emerging markets. VXUS covers 98% of the world's non-U.S. markets. The iShares Core MSCI Emerging Market ETF (IEMG) is another option that offers exposure to emerging markets.

REAL ESTATE

Real estate offers stable returns through rental income and profits from price appreciation. The cash flow from real estate provides ongoing, monthly income that is passive.

If you are thinking about investing in physical real estate, be sure to consult a Chartered Accountant (CA) who can supplement your research, help you with financing, and advise you on how to structure the ownership of the property.

A real estate investment trust (REIT) is an easy way for the average investor to gain exposure to the property market. REIT do a fairly good job of combating inflation. REITs are created when a corporation (or trust) uses investors' money to purchase and operate income properties. REITs hold property like office towers, apartment buildings, shopping centers, and hotels.

Unfortunately, REITs are not tax-efficient. Some of their payouts are considered "other income," which is fully taxable and not eligible for the dividend tax credit. Therefore, REITs are best held in a tax-sheltered account.

Vanguard REIT ETF (VNQ) is at the top of the list for broad, diversified exposure and a reasonable expense ratio.

Vanguard Global ex-U.S. Real Estate ETF (VNQI) provides a convenient way to get broad exposure across international REIT equity markets.

COMMODITIES

Commodities include precious metals (gold, silver, platinum, copper), energy (crude oil, gasoline, natural gas, heating oil), and agriculture (sugar, coffee, wheat, corn, soybeans).

Having some exposure to commodities is part of a well-diversified portfolio. Adding commodities to a retirement portfolio reduces overall portfolio risk and increases overall returns in the long-term.

Commodities are considered a hedge against inflation. Few assets benefit from rising inflation, particularly unexpected inflation, but commodity prices usually rise when inflation is accelerating. Commodities tend to bear a low to negative correlation to other asset classes, and at times commodities move opposite to stocks and bonds. At times, bear markets in stocks are accompanied by bull markets in commodities and vice versa.[3]

Investors are advised to allocate 5% to 10% of their portfolios to commodities. A study found that portfolio risk was reduced significantly when 10% or more of the portfolio was allocated to commodity futures.[4]

It's easy to add commodities to an investment portfolio through a broad commodity ETF or index fund. It's important to make sure commodity exposure is broad-based and not overly focused on a single commodity.

The Continuous Commodity Index Fund (GCC) is one of the most diversified choices. Other options are the

PowerShares DB Commodity Index Tracking Fund (DBC), United States Commodity Index Fund (USCI), Rogers International Commodity Index (RICI), and iShares S&P GSCI Commodity-Indexed Trust ETF (GSG).

Timber is another commodity to consider adding to an investment portfolio. It provides long-term investors with high returns and low volatility.

During the Great Depression, timber gained 233% while the price of stocks fell more than 70%. During the three worst market downturns of the 20th century (1911-1920, 1929-1941, and 1966-1981), timber outperformed the S&P 500.During the last session of high inflation in the U.S. (1973-1981), it was a good hedge, increasing by an average of 22% per year.

Expert investor Jeremy Grantham points to the fact that timber has risen 3% more than inflation for more than 90 years. During the next several years, he expects timber to have an inflation-adjusted return of 6%.Grantham considers timber "a perfect investment" for someone with a time horizon of 20 years or more. Timber REITs and ETFs give investors the ability to invest in timber.

Investors can choose between two ETFs that hold a broad portfolio of timber stocks: iShares S&P Global Timber& Forestry Index Fund (WOOD) and Guggenheim Timber ETF(CUT).

Another option is a timber real estate investment trust (REIT) such as Rayonier (RYN), Weyerhauser (WY), and Potlach (PCH).

FARMLAND

Farmland is the world's most valuable asset in a time of crisis. Farmland has outpaced both stocks and gold since 1970—total returns of U.S. farmland were more than 600%.

In the short-term, farmland has a degree of volatility which is determined by commodity prices, climate change, and insect infestations. However, there are many long-term factors that will drive up the prices of farmland, such as population growth, a finite supply of land, and increasing global demand for food.

Buying physical farmland is an option for wealthy investors. Most investors buy into a limited partnership or purchase land and have it professionally managed.

The closest an investor can get to owning a physical farm is through investing in a farmland real estate investment trust (REIT). Farmland REITs typically purchase farmland and then lease it to farmers. Some examples include Farmland Partners Inc. (FPI), Gladstone Land Corporation (LAND), and American Farmland (AFCO).

INFRASTRUCTURE

As roads, bridges, power and water facilities degenerate, the need to repair and upgrade them emerges. In developing countries, there is a need to build roads and facilities for increased industrialization.

Infrastructure investing has lower price volatility than equity investments, providing a steady return over the long-term. Historically, infrastructure investments have been lucrative. Many financial advisors suggest an allocation of 5-

10% of one's total investment portfolio to infrastructure ETFs. Some examples include iShares Global Infrastructure ETF (IGF), SPDR S&P Global Infrastructure ETF (GII), and DJ Brookfield Global Infrastructure ETF (TOLZ).

PRIVATE EQUITY

Private equity is an asset class consisting of equity securities and debt in private companies that are not publicly traded on a stock exchange. Private equity is typically considered a less volatile asset class that can offer both stable returns and relatively higher dividends.

You can purchase shares of an exchange-traded fund (ETF) that tracks an index of publicly traded companies that invest in private equities.

The PowerShares Global Listed Private Equity Portfolio (PSP) is the largest private equity ETF. It is the perfect option for investors looking for global exposure, as it provides access to private equity companies worldwide. Another option is the ProShares Global Listed Private Equity Portfolio (PEX).

MONEY MARKET

The Talmud teaches that money needs to be properly diversified in various asset classes, but you should also keep "one third at hand," (BavaMetzia 42a) meaning that you should keep some money "at hand" in cash reserve in the bank or in a money market.

It's essential to always keep some money in cash reserve for emergencies as well as for good investment opportunities that arise.

A high-interest savings account can be used for the purpose of having money readily available and accessible. Another option for keeping money at hand is the money market.

The money market is typically considered a safe place to put money. There are several money market instruments, such as treasury bills (T-Bills), certificates of deposit (CD), and commercial paper. You can easily access the money market through money market funds or through a money market bank account.

A money market account tends to pay a higher interest rate than a bank savings account. Money market accounts are insured by the Federal Deposit Insurance Corporation (FDIC).

Money market funds offered at a brokerage or investment firm, while considered relatively safe, are not insured by the FDIC.Money market funds are comparable to savings accounts in terms of liquidity.

TIPS

Treasury Inflation-Protected Securities, or TIPS, provide protection against inflation. They automatically go up in value when inflation rises.

Investors with a long-term time horizon may consider adding TIPS to the fixed-income portion of their portfolio. TIPS are a suitable substitute for the proportion of retirement funds someone would otherwise keep in cash. For most investors, it's advisable to allocate at least 10% of retirement assets to TIPS.

TIPS are best suited for a tax-deferred retirement account such as an IRA or 401(k) because when their value increases due to inflation they are regarded as taxable income by the Internal Revenue Service.

You can invest in TIPS through Vanguard Short-Term Inflation-Protected Securities ETF (VTIP).This fund protects investors from the eroding effect of inflation by investing in securities that seek to provide a "real" return. The fund invests in bonds that are backed by the full faith and credit of the federal government and whose principal is adjusted quarterly based on inflation.

The Vanguard Short-Term Inflation-Protected Securities Index Fund (VTIP) tracks the Barclays U.S. Treasury Inflation-Protected Securities (TIPS) 0-5 Year Index and invests in inflation-protected U.S. Treasury securities that have a remaining maturity of fewer than five years.

TAKE ACTION

AVERAGE INVESTORS

- Allocate a fair percentage of your investment portfolio to each asset class. Rebalance your investment portfolio annually and reinvest dividends or use a robo-advisor that does this for you.

- Ensure that stock and bond allocation is correct before deciding on the percentage of other asset classes to own in an investment portfolio .Age is one way to decide on stock and bond allocation.

CLEVER INVESTORS

- Make investing decisions based on economic studies and by consulting many investment advisors .Invest a higher percentage in asset classes with the potential for growth and a much lower percentage in asset classes with a risk of decline.

- Buy low and sell high during bear market recoveries when markets are cheap, as well as when investor sentiment is "fear."

CHAPTER TWO

CODE #2: DIVERSIFICATION

CODE:
Ya'akov became greatly afraid and distressed. He divided the
people, flocks, cattle and camels with him into two camps,
saying, "If 'Esav comes to the one camp and attacks it, at least
the camp that is left will escape."
Tanakh (CJB, Genesis 32:8-9)

DECODED:
A person shouldn't place all his money in a single position.
Midrash (Bereishit Rabbah 32:8)

You want diversification in each asset class you own. "Divide
your investments among many places, for you do not know
what risks might lie ahead." (Ecclesiastes 11:2)

There are many published financial academic studies on
the importance of diversification. Diversification does not
guarantee success, but it does reduce the risks of investing.
For the average investor, the easiest and most affordable way

to diversify in each asset class is through broad ETFs or index funds.

In the book, *A Random Walk Down Wall Street*, Burton G Malkiel documented the tiny odds of picking winning individual stocks.

John C. Bogle, the founder of Vanguard, provides investors with a winning strategy for long-term investing success. He recommends investing in low-cost, broad-market, no-load index funds or broad-market ETFs. For example: A total stock market ETF, a total bond market ETF, a total international ETF, an emerging markets ETF, and a broad commodity ETF.

The classic low-cost index fund is broadly diversified, holding many stocks, and operates with minimal expenses and high tax efficiency.

There are very few differences between owning classic index funds as opposed to owning commission-free ETFs. The major difference between an ETF and an index fund is that ETFs can be bought or sold at any time during the trading day, while index funds can be bought or sold only once a day.

Investing in index funds or ETFs is a winning strategy because they're broadly diversified, which eliminates individual stock risk. Bogle explains the wisdom behind this winning strategy in the June 2014 issue of AAII Journal:

Imagine a circle representing 100% of the U.S. stock market, with each stock in there by its market weight. Then take out 30% of that circle. Those stocks are owned by people who index directly through index funds. The remaining 70% are owned by people who index collectively. By definition, they own the exact same portfolio as the indexers do in aggregate, so they will capture the same gross return as the direct indexers. But by trading back and forth, trying to beat one another, they will inevitably lose by the amount of their transaction costs, the amount of the advisory fees they pay, and the amount of all those mutual fund management costs they incur: marketing costs, processing, technology investments, everything. When we look at the big picture of the costs of investing, including sales loads as well as expense ratios and cash drag, it is a foregone conclusion that active investors, in aggregate, will underperform index investors. It's the mathematics. Borrowing a phrase from Louis Brandeis: It's the relentless rules of humble arithmetic. The 30% of investors who own index funds capture almost all of the market's return. In a 7% return market, indexing should deliver approximately 6.95% to investors. (A typical Vanguard all-market index fund charges 0.05%.) The remainder—those who are trading back and forth, hiring managers, and all that kind of thing—will incur costs, in round numbers, of about 2% per year. So, the indexers are going to capture pretty close to a 7% return in a 7% market, while the active investors, who also collectively own the index, are getting the same 7% gross return minus about 2% for all those fees and costs, a net return of 5%. It is definitional tautology that the indexers win and the traders lose.

BEAT THE MARKET

People pay investment managers a lot of money to beat the market. The skills and expertise of fund managers are supposed to give them the ability to select stocks and bonds that perform better than benchmarks such as the Dow or S&P 500. However, very few professional investors are able to beat the market.

Evidence consistently shows that the majority of individual investors, mutual funds, hedge funds, and venture capital funds underperform their risk-adjusted benchmarks every year, and especially over the long-term.

Studies of fund managers, active traders, and other institutional investors have failed to find consistent outperformance that wasn't caused by either luck or being in the right part of the market at the right time. One study reports: "The trend of a large percentage of managers failing to outperform their benchmarks over a longer-term horizon remains consistent."[5]

In a study of more than 24,000 mutual funds and ETFs, Nerd Wallet finds that actively managed mutual funds turned in an asset-weighted average return of 6.5% over the decade, compared to 7.3% for the passively managed index products. These results may have more to do with high fees rather than poor management skills. The study explains: "Active managers earn 0.12% higher annual returns than index investors before fees, but because they charge an average fee of 1.07%, much higher than the average index fee of only 0.15%, active investors are left with 1.10% less than index investors despite their manager earnings superior returns."

The SPIVA Scorecard keeps a report of the difference between active versus passive investing. According to the Year-End 2014 S&P Dow Jones Indices scorecard, 86% of active large-cap fund managers failed to beat their benchmarks over a one-year period. Small-cap active managers have been consistently underperforming the benchmark—it's the category where the highest percentages of managers (91.81%) have underperformed. The S&P 500 returned 13.69% in 2014. Returns were 32.39% in 2013 and

16% in 2012. Over five- and 10-year periods, 88.65% and 82.07% of large-cap managers failed to perform better than the benchmark—the S&P 500 is one of the most commonly used benchmarks for the overall U.S. stock market.

David Snowball, the founder of MutualFundObserver.com, said, "The industry is about making profit for the fund adviser and fund advisers make profits by drawing and holding assets, and the way you draw and hold assets is by not scaring people. So if you can get a couple of decent years together and a decent story and then slide quietly into mediocrity, it's a recipe for success for your fund company and a recipe for disappointment for investors."

Actively managed funds can beat market averages at times, but the odds are that managers will not be able to sustain those results. "The bigger the fund, the worse the performance," said Thomas Howard, director of research at AthenaInvest. He advises, "Instead of looking for the mostskilled managers, look for funds that impose the least portfolio tax, and when those burdens start to rise as the fund becomes successful and grows, there comes a point where you get out and move on." If you choose not to do that, then buy passive index funds and don't worry about beating the market.

Passive funds (index funds or ETFs) aim to match market averages. They have lower fees because the composition is already defined.

Investing should not be viewed as a casino game in which you either win big or lose big. Fred Schwed Jr., author of *Where Are the Customers' Yachts?* said, "Speculation is an effort, probably unsuccessful, to turn a little money into a lot. Investment is an effort, which should be successful, to prevent a lot of money from becoming a little."

Professional investor Benjamin Graham states, "The individual investor should act consistently as an investor and not as a speculator."

SET IT AND FORGET IT

Once you set up a solid retirement portfolio, you must "forget it" and stay the course when you are hit with recessions or declines. However, this is easier said than done for most people.

Behavioral finance provides explanations for why people make irrational financial decisions. All humans are irrational and subject to wild emotional swings leading to poor performance in the markets. Understanding behavioral finance will help investors to make better, less emotional decisions.

Economies are cyclical, and the markets have shown that they always recover. Make sure you are a part of those recoveries. "You get recessions; you have stock market declines. If you don't understand that's going to happen, then you're not ready, you won't do well in the markets," said successful professional investor Peter Lynch.

The Torah says, "There will be seven years of abundance throughout the whole land…but afterwards, there will come seven years of famine." (CJB, Genesis 41:29, 30) There is an economic cycle—not always seven years—of abundance (bull markets) and famine (bear markets). The Tanakh suggests, "In the day of prosperity be joyful, and in the day of adversity consider; God hath made even the one as well as the other." (JPS, Ecclesiastes 7:14) Successful investing requires common sense and rational decisions not based on emotions. Warren Buffet advises: "Making monthly investments in a low-cost index fund makes a lot of sense." The Tanakh says, "Wealth gotten by vanity shall be diminished, but he that gathereth little by little shall increase." (JPS, Proverbs 13:11) Successful investing also requires plenty of patience. "Investing should be more like watching paint dry or watching grass grow. If you want excitement, take $800 and go to Las Vegas," said American economist, Paul Samuelson.

If you are focused on investing to accumulate great wealth, create two portfolios: A "set-it-and-forget-it" retirement portfolio of broad ETFs or index funds, and a separate "play portfolio" in which you try to pick winning investments that you believe have the potential for a high Return On Investment (ROI).

Occasionally, picking winners will result in the accumulation of great wealth. For example, a portfolio consisting of 100% Apple stock (AAPL) within a time frame of 35 years would result in a ROI of 31,590.90%. An investment of $990 in Apple stock (AAPL) on December 12, 1980 would have generated over $300,000 on July 24, 2015 after stock splits and excluding dividends. Very clever investors such as Warren Buffett, William O'Neil, Ralph Wanger, Thomas Rowe Price, Jr., and John Neff, among others, are able to pick winners at times, but not always. The very clever investor spends plenty of time, effort, study, and exhaustive research picking individual stocks or other investments for their "play portfolio." They select individual stocks based on true value, a topic covered in the next chapter.

TAKE ACTION

AVERAGE INVESTORS
- Build a retirement investment portfolio consisting of low-cost, broad-market, no-load index funds or broad-market, commission-free ETFs.

- Set-it-and-forget-it. Once you set up a solid retirement portfolio, you must "forget it" and stay the course when hit with recessions or declines.

CLEVER INVESTORS
- Create two portfolios: A "set-it-and-forget-it" retirement portfolio of broad ETFs or index funds, and a separate "play portfolio" in which you try to pick winning investments that you believe have the potential for a high ROI.

- The very clever investor spends plenty of time, effort, study, and exhaustive research to choose individual stocks or other investments they hope are winning picks.

CHAPTER THREE

CODE #3: TRUE VALUE

CODE:
And if thou sell aught unto thy neighbour, or buy of thy
neighbour's hand, ye shall not wrong one another.
Tanakh (JPS, Leviticus 25:14)

DECODED:
And if thou sell aught unto thy neighbour...ye shall not
deceive.
Talmud (Baba Mezi'a 51a)

In Roman Law, price was a matter to be determined entirely
by free contract. It was left to the buyer and the seller to agree
upon the price at their own risk. Julius Paulus, a jurist of the
third century, stated that, in buying and selling, a man has a
right to purchase for a small price that which is really valuable
and to sell at a higher price that which is less valuable, and
each may seek to cheat and take advantage of the other.
According to Jewish Law, this is unethical and wrong. "If you

sell anything to your neighbor or buy anything from him, neither of you is to exploit the other." (CJB, Leviticus 25:14)

STOCK PRICES

The issue of deceptive information and the exploiting of the buyer of a stock is present today. Only the seller of a stock knows the true value of what they are selling. The buyer of a stock expects that the stock they are purchasing will only increase in value.

At times, the buyer purchases financial assets that are of little value and that don't increase in value or worse yet, decrease in value. Investors who buy individual stocks based on false information frequently deal with massive losses.

Seth Klarman's book, *Margin of Safety*, reflects the renowned value hedge fund manager's views of individual stock picking formulas:

Some investment formulas involve technical analysis, in which past stock-price movements are considered predictive of future prices. Other formulas incorporate investment fundamentals such as price-to-earnings (P/E) ratio, ratios, price-to-book-value ratios, sales or profits growth rates, dividend yields, and the prevailing level of interest rates. Despite the enormous effort that has been put into devising such formulas, none has been proven to work. One simplistic, backward-looking formula employed by some investors is to buy stocks with low P/E ratio. The idea is that by paying a low multiple of earnings, an investor is buying an out-of-favor bargain. In reality, investors who follow such a formula are essentially driving by looking only in the rear-view mirror. Stocks with a low P/E ratio are often depressed because the market price has already discounted the prospect of a sharp fall in earnings. Investors who buy such stocks may soon find that the P/E ratio has risen because earnings have declined. The financial markets are far too complex to be incorporated into a formula. Investors would be much better off to redirect the time and effort committed to devising formulas into fundamental analysis of specific investment opportunities.

STOCK MANIPULATION

Stock manipulation, insider trading, misstatements on a public company's financial reports, and lying to corporate auditors are rampant deceptive practices that cause investors to incur losses on their investments. Corporate executives can and do manipulate stock prices regularly for their own benefit.

The Securities Investor Protection Corporation (SIPC) reports that the FTC, the FBI, and state securities regulators estimate that investment fraud in the United States ranges from $10–$40 billion annually.

In his book, *The Number: How the Drive for Quarterly Earnings Corrupted Wall Street and Corporate America*, Alex Berenson explains how publicly traded companies deceived their shareholders and manipulated quarterly earnings during the record bull run of the 1990s and the subsequent crash.

The quarterly earnings report is a quarterly filing made by public companies to report their performance. Earnings reports include net income, earnings per share, earnings from continuing operations, and net sales.

The quarterly earnings report was used by analysts and investors as a convenient tool for their investment decisions during the 1990s. This led every fund manager and investor to buy the same stocks, leaving the undervalued stocks to clever investors such as Warren Buffett.

Stock prices are also manipulated because of large investors. Those that hold billions of shares of a stock buy shares when prices are falling, and sell shares when prices are rising. Such large positions cannot be traded without manipulating the share price. When a large investor sells a large position of a stock, it pushes prices lower.

The average investor will avoid being exploited by stock manipulators simply by holding index funds or ETF's. Clever investors will use certain principles when trying to pick winning stocks.

VALUE INVESTING

There is no "perfect investing formula," but there are certain principles that the clever investor employs when trying to pick winning individual stocks to make huge profits(Learn how to properly pick stocks by referring to Appendix C: Picking Individual Stocks).

The Talmud teaches, "Engaging in business brings more profit than you can do." Engaging in business, such as through picking winning stocks, brings more profit than working hard for money as the majority of people do.

It's possible to pick winners by employing value investing. Benjamin Graham and Warren Buffett are two examples of successful value investors. Warren Buffett became the second wealthiest person in the world through the application of value investing principles to pick winning individual stocks.

Benjamin Graham taught that you can minimize your odds of errors by never overpaying regardless of how exciting an investment appears.

However, value investing is a challenging endeavor that few are able to master. All investors are advised to hold two portfolios: A retirement portfolio, and a separate "play portfolio" in which to pick individual stocks.

Success in value investing requires the utmost patience and discipline. "To achieve satisfactory investment results is easier than most people realize; to achieve superior results is harder than it looks," said Benjamin Graham in his book, *The Intelligent Investor.*

Research shows that value investing can work over longer time periods (five or more years). Value investing is less reliable over shorter time horizons because of factors such as short-term price momentum.

The fundamentals of the business are taken into account by a successful value investor. Weak fundamentals can make certain stocks cheap for a reason.

Speculators are the opposite of value investors. They are unconcerned with the fundamentals of a company and hope to make a quick gain.

Value investors can succeed by following the principles taught in the Tanakh. "Without deliberation, plans go wrong." (CJB, Proverbs 15:22) "One rushing to get rich will not go unpunished. He who is greedy rushes after riches, not knowing that want will overtake him." (CJB, Proverbs 28:20, 22) "All who rush in arrive only at want." (CJB, Proverbs 21:5) "The thoughtless believeth every word; but the prudent man looketh well to his going." (JPS, Proverbs 14:15)

Many people have made bad financial investments because of pride. The Tanakh warns, "Pride goes before destruction, and arrogance before failure." (CJB, Proverbs 16:18) "Before being ruined, a person's heart is proud." (CJB, Proverbs 18:12)

NUMBER OF STOCKS TO OWN

The optimal amount of individual value stocks to own in a well-balanced "play portfolio" is 20 or 30stocks. Warren Buffett said, "Wide diversification is only required when investors do not understand what they are doing." In other words, if you own too many individual stocks, you might not lose much, but you won't gain much either.

A study found that the average standard deviation (risk) of a portfolio of one stock was 49.2%, while increasing the number of stocks in the well-balanced portfolio could reduce the portfolio's standard deviation to a maximum of 19.2%. However, a portfolio of 20 stocks reduced risk to about 20%. Therefore, the additional stocks from 20 to 1,000 reduced the portfolio's risk by only about 0.8%, while the first 20 stocks reduced the portfolio's risk by 29.2%.

Buying 20 stocks does not equate to optimum diversification. Diversification requires buying investments that are uncorrelated—investments that move in different directions during different times—and that are distinct from each other, whether by company, size, industry, sector, or country.

A well-balanced "play portfolio" with approximately 20 individual stocks reduces the maximum amount of market risk.

TAKE ACTION

AVERAGE INVESTORS
- There is potential to be exploited on an individual stock purchase. The average investor will avoid being exploited by stock manipulators simply by buying and holding index funds or ETF's.

CLEVER INVESTORS
- Hold two portfolios: A retirement portfolio and a separate "play portfolio" in which one can try to pick winning stocks.

- Study, research, and put time and effort into picking winning individual stocks through value investing. Select and hold at least 20 stocks in your "play portfolio."

CHAPTER FOUR

CODE #4: TITHING

CODE:

Though I have afflicted thee, I will afflict thee no more.

Tanakh (JPS, Nahum 1:12)

DECODED:

Even a poor man who himself subsists on charity should give charity. If he does that, [Heaven] will not again inflict poverty upon him.

Talmud (Gittin 7b)

Tzedakah, the Jewish term for helping the poor, is often translated as "charity." Giving tzedakah is an obligation in Judaism, a duty that cannot be ignored even by those who are themselves in need. The Talmud says, "Even a poor person who receives tzedakah must, in turn, give tzedakah." (Gittin 7b)Jewish sage Rav Yosef taught that the Tanakh verse, "I will afflict you no more," (JPS, Nahum 1:12) means that a person who gives charity "will no longer be afflicted with poverty."

THE #1 COMMANDMENT

There are 613 mitzvot (commandments) in the Torah. Most of the Torah's 613 commandments are for the benefit of others and society as a whole, but tzedakahis a command that benefits the giver even more so than the receiver. According to Jewish tradition, the benefit of giving to the poor is so great that a beggar actually does the giver a favor by allowing a person the opportunity to perform tzedakah. The Midrash says, "The blessing of tzedakah is greater for the person who gives than for the person who receives." (Leviticus Rabbah 34:10)The most important commandment given in the Torah is to give charity. (Deuteronomy 15:11) Jewish sages have taught that giving charity is equal to all the other commandments combined, making it the number-one commandment.

The Old Covenant contained in the Torah promised prosperity, among other things, as a reward for obedience. "Observe the words of this covenant and obey them; so that you can make everything you do prosper." (CJB, Deuteronomy 29:9)

Those who don't obey the number-one commandment in the Torah may even come under a curse of poverty. God says that there is "a curse on anyone who does not pay attention to the words of this covenant." (CJB, Jeremiah 11:3)

The Talmud says, "Tzedakah is as important as all the other commandments put together." (Baba Batra 9a) Therefore, simply following this one command can result in prosperity. "He who gives to the poor will lack nothing, but he who hides his eyes will get curses in plenty." (CJB, Proverbs 28:27)

GUIDELINES OF TZEDAKAH

Most traditional Jews give Maaser Kesafim, one-tenth of one's income, also known as tithing. Rabbinic scholars set a standard that at a minimum every person is obligated to give 10% of their annual income or realized gains.

At the same time, a cap of 20% of annual income is placed on giving. Shulchan Aruch states that there are three levels of giving. A generous person will give 20% of his assets to charity. An average person will give 10%. Anything below 10% is considered stingy, although it is not strictly forbidden.

Those who are poor may give less, but must still give to the extent they are able; however, no person should give so much that they become poor and dependent on charity themselves.

All recurring income is tithed annually, but assets are tithed only once, not annually. It is recommended to give "the firstfruits of all your income" (CJB, Proverbs 3:9, 10) meaning to tithe first before making any bill payments but after payment of taxes.

Taxes themselves do not fulfill our obligation to give tzedakah, even though a significant portion of tax revenues in many countries is used to provide for the poor and needy.

Tithing is taken off net profits. A person is not obligated to give tzedakah from unrealized gains. Thus, if one's financial assets appreciate in value, there is no obligation to give until the asset is sold, resulting in realized gains. In addition, a person does not need to give tzedakahif the principal is still at risk. Thus, a speculative investment that is currently paying out returns would not be considered suitable until the original investment is recovered.[7]

BENEFITS OF TZEDAKAH

Tithing is mentioned more than once in the Talmud, indicating how important this code is for wealth creation. The Talmud advises, "Give tithes so that thou mayest become wealthy" (Shabbath 119a) and "Tithe so that you will become rich." (Taanit 9a)

Every investment, every financial decision, every effort to earn money has the potential for failure or success. The Mishna advises, "Pray to him to whom all wealth and property belong [to God], because every craft contains the potentialities for both poverty and wealth. Neither poverty nor wealth is due to the craft, but all depends on merit." (Kiddushin 82a)

The book *Jewish Wisdom for Business Success* says, "Try to build your merit. This involves praying, giving to charity, and helping others. The more merit you are able to garner, the more Divine energy you attract and the more successful you will be in every area of life." The Talmud says, "The wealthy merit wealth because they give tithes, as it is written: Asser te'asser [which means], give tithes [asser] so that thou mayest become wealthy [tith'asser]." (Shabbat 119a)

The Talmud tells us that it is permitted to "test" God to learn whether we will become wealthy through tithing. The Talmud tells us that it is forbidden to test God in all cases, except for tithing, because it is written, "Bring the whole tithe into the store-house, that there may be food in my house, and test me with this, says the Lord of hosts, if I will not open for you the windows of heaven, and pour you out a blessing, until it is beyond enough." (Malachi 3:10) "Beyond enough" means "until your lips are tired from saying enough." (Taanit 9a)

The guarantee of wealth is also applicable only if the entire tithe is given to those in poverty who require these funds to sustain themselves with the basic necessities of life. The obligation to tithe can also be fulfilled by giving money to charities, health care institutions, places of worship, educational institutions, or beggars.

John D. Rockefeller, regarded by many as the wealthiest man in history and worth over $300 billion in today's figures, said, "I never would have been able to tithe the first million dollars I ever made if I had not tithed my first salary, which was $1.50 per week." Rockefeller tithed on all of his reoccurring earnings for his entire life. As his wealth grew, so did his charitable contributions.

When you tithe, you show your trust in God as your source and you will be blessed. (Psalm 40:4) Your job, business, investments, assets, or wherever you're getting money from is not your source. They can fail or disappear in an instant. Therefore, it's important not to become proud and dependent on your own abilities. (Proverbs 11:2)

"You will think to yourself, 'My own power and the strength of my own hand have gotten me this wealth.' No, you are to remember Adonai your God, because it is he who is giving you the power to get wealth, in order to confirm his covenant, which he swore to your ancestors, as is happening even today." How do you remember God as your source? By tithing on all your reoccurring income and realized gains.

OBLIGATIONS OF TZEDAKAH

We have an obligation to make sure the funds we give are being used properly. We must do due diligence and investigate the legitimacy of a charity before donating to it. We can also refuse to give if we have doubts about a beggar's situation.

There are many people who ask for charity but who have no genuine need; if we know that our funds aren't going to be used wisely, we can refuse to give. The Talmud states that we don't need to give to all who ask. (Kesuvos 68a) The existence of frauds and cheaters diminishes our liability for failing to give to all who ask.

The Talmud suggests petitioning God for help in giving to the right cause and the right people. God will send people who are fitting recipients of charity so that you will be rewarded for assisting them. You want to avoid giving to unsuitable recipients and getting no reward for your efforts.

"Sovereign of the Universe, even at the time when they conquer their evil inclination and seek to do charity before Thee, cause them to stumble through men who are not fitting recipients so that they should receive no reward for assisting them." (Baba Bathra 9b)

Besides the obligation to give to a worthy cause and worthy recipients, we need to avoid becoming in need of charity ourselves. If a person is unemployed, they should humbly take any work that is available, even if they think it is beneath their skills, talents, and dignity. The Talmud says that "idleness leads to idiocy." (Kethubos 59b) Rabbi Yehuda and Rabbi Shimon stated: "Great is labour, for it honors the worker." (Talmud, Nedarim 49b)

Both sages would purposely carry burdens on their shoulders because they wanted their students to see that manual labor is to be respected. "A person should love work and not hate it." (Avot D'Rabbi Nosson 11:1)

LEVELS OF TZEDAKAH

Certain types of tzedakah are considered more worthy than others. The Talmud says, "He who gives a small coin to a poor man obtains six blessings, and he who addresses to him words of comfort obtains eleven blessings." (Baba Bathra 9b)The Talmud describes different levels of tzedakah. The levels of charity, from the least beneficial to the most beneficial, are:

- Giving begrudgingly
- Giving less than you should, but giving it cheerfully
- Giving after being asked
- Giving before being asked
- Giving when you do not know the recipient's identity, but the recipient knows your identity
- Giving when you know the recipient's identity, but the recipient doesn't know your identity
- Giving when neither party knows the other's identity
- Enabling the recipient to become self-reliant

The lowest level of tzedakah is giving grudgingly, and the highest level is enabling a recipient to become self-reliant. The Tanakh explains how important it is to give freely: "You must give to him, and you are not to be grudging when you give to him. If you do this, Adonai your God will bless you in all your work, in everything you undertake." (CJB, Deuteronomy 15:10)"Wealth and riches are in his house...He distributes freely, he gives to the poor." (CJB, Psalm 112:3, 9) Jewish sage Rabbi Abahu explains that "If you see a person distributing his money to charity, know that his assets will increase."

BONUS BENEFITS OF TZEDAKAH

The return a person gets from giving to charity is not just an increase in assets, but also enormously valuable things that money can never buy, such as a long life and protection from an early death. "Long life is in her right hand, riches and honor in her left." (CJB, Proverbs 3:16) The Talmud says that "charity saves from death." (Baba Bathra 10a) The following story is found in the Talmud (Tract Aboth):

It happened that a pious man who used to spend much in charity, while aboard a ship encountered a great storm, and the ship foundered. Rabbi Aqiba saw him go down. Rabbi Aqiba then encountered him at another time. Rabbi Aqiba said to him: "Did you not sink into the sea?" He answered: "Yeah." Rabbi Aqiba then asked, "Who brought thee out of the sea?" He answered: "The charities that I have given have saved me from the sea. When I went down in the deep, I heard the noise of the waves. It seemed to me that they said to each other: This man has done charity all his days and they actually threw me on land." Rabbi Aqiba then arose and said, "Blessed be the Lord the God of Israel, who has chosen the words of the Torah and the words of the sages, for they are preserved everlastingly. As it is written 'Cast thy bread upon the face of the waters; for after many days wilt thou find it again' (Ecclesiastes 11:1). It is written again (Proverbs 10:2): 'Charity will deliver from death.'"

TAKE ACTION

THE AVERAGE INVESTOR
- An average investor will give 10% of their realized investment gains to charity. They do not give begrudgingly. They know that giving charity results in an increase in assets as well as a long life and protection from an early death.

- An average investor saving and investing for a comfortable retirement will avoid becoming in need of charity. If they are unemployed, they will humbly take any work that is available, even if they think it is beneath their skills, talents, and dignity.

THE CLEVER INVESTOR
- A generous, clever investor will give 20% of their realized investment gains to charity. They give their charity in secret and before being asked to give. At the highest level of giving, they enable a recipient to become self-reliant.

- The clever investor thoroughly investigates the legitimacy of a charity before donating to it. They refuse to give if they have doubts about a beggar's situation.

APPENDIX A: BUILD A PORTFOLIO

STEP ONE

Select and open an account with a well-reviewed investment broker:

www.vanguard.com

www.fidelity.com

www.schwab.com

www.etrade.com

www.interactivebrokers.com

www.firstrade.com

www.mbtrading.com

www.tradeking.com

www.tdameritrade.com

www.merrilledge.com

www.betterment.com

www.wealthfront.com

www.wealthsimple.com

STEP TWO

Construct a well-diversified "retirement portfolio" of broad ETF's or index funds in seven to ten asset classes: domestic stocks, international developed market stocks, emerging market stocks, bonds, commodities, real estate, timberland, agriculture, infrastructure, or private equity.

STEP THREE

Rebalance your portfolio annually to bring the asset allocation percentage back in line with the desired allocation percentage or use a robo-advisor that offers automatic rebalancing and dividend reinvesting. Robo-advisors such as Betterment (www.betterment.com), Wealthfront (www.wealthfront.com), and Wealth Simple (www.wealthsimple.com)are the suitable automated investment platforms.

STEP FOUR (OPTIONAL)

Construct a "play portfolio" separate from your "retirement portfolio" for selecting stocks that you believe are winners based on value investing principles. It's ideal to use a different broker for your "play portfolio" so that there is no interference with your retirement portfolio. For example, your "set-it-and-forget-it" retirement portfolio would be with Vanguard (www.vanguard.com) while your "play portfolio" would be with eTrade (www.etrade.com).

APPENDIX B: SAMPLE PORTFOLIOS

TALMUDIC PORTFOLIO

The Talmud suggests that "A person should always divide his money into three: one third in land, one third in commerce, and one third at hand [in reserve]." (Bava Metzia 42a)

The Maharsha (a commentary on the stories of the Talmud) explains the financial logic of this asset allocation. Land is safe because it can't lose all its value. Commerce has the highest return, but also the highest risk. Finally, some money must be left "at hand," meaning readily available and liquid.

"Land" can refer to REITs, timberland, farmland, or agriculture. "Commerce" refers to stocks or private equity. Money "at hand" refers to bonds, treasury bills, money markets, or an FDIC-insured bank.

The Talmudic Portfolio is simple and straightforward, requiring only four ETF purchases: 34% land (17% timber and 17% REIT), 33% commerce (total world stock market), and 33% in reserve (total bond market).

Commerce (33%)
Vanguard Total World Stock ETF (VT)

Land: Timber (17%) and REIT (17%)
Vanguard REIT ETF (VNQ)
iShares Global Timber& Forestry ETF (WOOD)

Reserve (33%)
Vanguard Total Bond Market ETF (BND)

ADVANCED TALMUDIC PORTFOLIO

Roger C. Gibson, investmentadvisor and asset allocation expert, uses a more advanced version of the Talmudic Portfolio. His firm is one of the only firms which takes into account the Bible verse from Ecclesiastes 11:2: "Divide your portion to seven, or even to eight, for you do not know what misfortune may occur on the earth."

Gibson takes into account the advice of the Talmud to always divide his money into three: one third in land, one third in commerce, and one third at hand [in reserve]." (BavaMetzia 42a) The modern-day version of the Talmud's advice to divide your money into three portions is done through bonds, stocks, and hard assets.

The seven broad asset classes include short-term bond funds, U.S. bonds, international bonds, U.S. stocks, international stocks, real estate, and commodities. The percentage of 30% bonds, 40% stocks, and 30% hard assets can be adjusted according to one's risk tolerance.

Short-Term Bond ETF (10%)
Vanguard Short-Term Bond fund (BSV)

U.S. Bond ETF (10%)
Vanguard Total Bond Market ETF (BND)

International Bond ETF (10%)
Vanguard Total International Bond ETF (BNDX)

U.S. Stock ETF(20%)
Vanguard Total Stock Market ETF (VTI)

International Stocks (20%)
Vanguard FTSE All-World ex-US ETF (VEU)

Real Estate (25%)
Vanguard REIT ETF (VNQ)

Commodities (5%)
PowerShares DB Commodity Index Tracking Fund (DBC)

SIMPLE TALMUDIC PORTFOLIO

There is a very simple Talmudic portfolio for people who
don't want to maintain their own allocation to stocks and
bonds. It consists of a one-fund approach. You never have to
rebalance a balanced fund—it's done for you automatically.

The Vanguard Balanced Index (VBINX) is a single
balanced index fund in which the allocation to stocks and

bonds is held constant by the fund company. The fund invests roughly 60% in stocks and 40% in bonds by tracking two indexes that represent broad barometers for the U.S. equity and U.S. taxable bond markets. The Vanguard STAR Fund (VGSTX) is a very similar option and could be used in place of the Vanguard Balanced Index. However, while both of these funds cover commerce and reserve, you will still need to add land investment into the allocation mix with assets such as farmland, REIT, or timberland.

The iShares Balanced Growth CorePortfolio Index ETF (CBN)is a simple way to gain exposure to a portfolio of ETFs that is diversified by asset classes and across global regions. It holds assets such as equity, fixed income, real estate, and agriculture.

INVESTING CODE PORTFOLIO

The Investing Code portfolio divides a portfolio into eight asset classes following the wise advice of the Tanakh to diversify broadly into many asset classes (seven or eight). "Divide a portion into seven, yea, even into eight." (JPS, Ecclesiastes 11:2)

Asset classes include domestic stocks, international/emerging market stocks, bonds, real estate, commodities, farmland, timberland, and infrastructure.

Commerce allocation is 40% (U.S. stock, international/emerging stock), reserve allocation is 30% (bonds), and land allocation is 30% (REIT, commodity, farmland, timber, infrastructure). Allocation can be modified according to risk tolerance.

Stock ETF (20%)
Vanguard Total Stock Market ETF (VTI)

International/Emerging Markets ETF(20%)
Vanguard FTSE All-World ex-US ETF (VEU)

Bond ETF (30%)
Vanguard Total Bond Market ETF (BND)

Real Estate ETF (10%)
Vanguard REIT ETF (VNQ)

Commodity ETF (5%)
Continuous Commodity Index Fund (GCC)

Farmland ETF (5%)
Farmland Partners Inc. REIT (FPI)

Timber ETF (5%)
iShares Global Timber& Forestry ETF (WOOD)

Infrastructure ETF (5%)
iShares Global Infrastructure ETF (IGF)

ADVANCED INVESTING CODE PORTFOLIO

The advanced version of The Investing Code Portfolio has ten asset classes, including domestic stocks, international stocks, emerging market stocks, bonds, real estate, commodities, farmland, timberland, infrastructure, and private equity.

Commerce allocation is 40% (U.S. stock, international and emerging stock), reserve allocation is 30% (bonds), and land allocation is 30% (REIT, commodity, farmland, timber, infrastructure). Allocation can be modified according to risk tolerance.

This asset allocation model is especially powerful if you practice annual rebalancing and dividend reinvesting which will cause you to buy low and sell high automatically.

Stock ETF (10%)
Vanguard Total Stock Market ETF (VTI)

International ETF (10%)
Vanguard Total International Stock ETF (VXUS)

Emerging Market Stock ETF (10%)
iShares Edge MSCI Minimum Volatility Emerging Markets (XMM)

Private Equity ETF (10%)
Global Listed Private Equity ETF (PEX)

Bond ETF (30%)
Vanguard Total Bond Market ETF (BND)

Real Estate ETF (10%)
Vanguard REIT ETF (VNQ)

Commodity ETF (5%)
Continuous Commodity Index Fund (GCC)

Farmland ETF (5%)
Farmland Partners Inc. REIT (FPI)

Timber ETF (5%)
iShares Global Timber& Forestry ETF (WOOD)

Infrastructure ETF (5%)
iShares Global Infrastructure ETF (IGF)

APPENDIX C: PICKING INDIVIDUAL STOCKS

Behavioral finance explains why human psychology and behavior causes people to make irrational financial decisions that can push stock prices far below their intrinsic value.

Value investing is all about buying stocks at a discount to what they are actually worth and having them appreciate in price. Value investing is a helpful tool in deciding on which stocks to buy.

Value investing is primarily concerned with the fundamentals of a company's business rather than its stock price or market factors affecting its price.

Value investing consists of buying undervalued stocks at prices significantly below their intrinsic value. Market price is known, but the intrinsic value must be estimated subjectively. Intrinsic value is a function of the long-term profitability of a company and is affected by numerous factors.

Benjamin Graham is the "Father of Value Investing" and was Warren Buffett's teacher. Benjamin Graham recommended a practical tool for evaluating a stock's intrinsic value.

Graham's Updated Intrinsic Value Formula

$$V = \{EPS \times (8.5 + 2g) \times 4.4\} / Y$$

V: Intrinsic Value

EPS: the company's last 12-month earnings per share

8.5: the constant represents the appropriate P-E ratio for a no-growth company as proposed by Graham

g: the company's long-term (five years) earnings growth estimate

4.4: the average yield of high-grade corporate bonds in 1962, when this model was introduced

Y: the current yield on 20 year AAA corporate bonds.

The Intrinsic Value Formula for evaluating a stock's intrinsic value should be just one factor in making a buy decision. The investor must take into account many other factors.

Graham recommended using Standard & Poor's rating system and selecting companies that have an S&P Earnings and Dividend Rating of B or better. The S&P rating system ranges from D to A+.

Graham advised buying companies with Total Debt to Current Asset ratios of less than 1.10. Total Debt to Current Asset ratios can be found in data supplied by Standard & Poor's, Value Line, or other investment services.

Check the Current Ratio (current assets divided by current liabilities) to find companies with ratios over 1.50. This is a common ratio provided by many investment services.

Find companies with positive earnings per share growth during the past five years with no earnings deficits. Earnings need to be higher in the most recent year than five years ago. Avoid companies with earnings deficits during the past five years.

Invest in companies with price to earnings per share (P/E) ratios of 9.0 or less. Finding a company with a low P/E ratio usually eliminates high growth companies, which should be evaluated using growth investing techniques.

Find companies with price to book value (P/BV) ratios less than 1.20. P/E ratios can sometimes be misleading. P/BV ratios are calculated by dividing the current price by the most recent book value per share for a company. Book value provides a good indication of the underlying value of a company. Investing in stocks selling near or below their book value is wise.

Invest in companies that are currently paying dividends. Investing in undervalued companies requires you to patiently wait for other investors to discover the bargains you have already discovered. If the company pays a decent dividend, you can collect dividends while you wait patiently for your stock to go from undervalued to overvalued.

To buy an undervalued stock that is worth more than it is currently trading you must thoroughly research the company and not just buy a stock because its ratios look good or because its price has recently dropped. It's very important to find out why a stock is selling at a bargain price.

In his book, *The Little Book of Value Investing*, Christopher H. Browne recommends asking a series of questions about a company. Can the company increase its revenue by raising prices? Increasing sales? Lowering expenses? Selling or closing unprofitable divisions? Growing the company? Who are the company's competitors and how strong are they?

Value investing is not an exact science. It's important to realize that you can't just plug some numbers into a software program to determine the best stocks.

APPENDIX D: RECOMMENDED READING

Bernstein, W. (2002).*The Four Pillars of Investing: Lessons for Building a Winning Portfolio*. New York, NY: McGraw-Hill

Merriman, P. (2011). *Financial Fitness Forever*. McGraw-Hill Education.

Bogle, J. (2009). *The Little Book of Common Sense Investing: The Only Way to Guarantee Your Fair Share of Stock Market Returns*. Hoboken, NJ: Wiley & Sons.

Greenblatt, J. (2008). *The Little Book That Still Beats the Market*. Hoboken, NJ: Wiley & Sons.

Graham, B. (2006). *The Intelligent Investor: The Definitive Book on Value Investing*. HarperBusiness.

Rogers, J. (2004). *Hot Commodities: How Anyone Can Invest Profitably in the World's Best Market*. Random House.

ABOUT THE AUTHOR

Howard Ward Charles, who publishes as H. W. Charles, studied Biblical Studies and is the recipient of several academic awards. He has a great interest in Hebrew, Jewish philosophy, and interpretation of the Jewish Bible. He published *The Money Code: Become a Millionaire with the Ancient Jewish Code* in October 2012. The book is written in a straightforward manner so as to help all benefit from the financial wisdom found in ancient Jewish texts. H. W. Charles published *The Investment Code: Sacred Jewish Wisdom for the Wise Investor* in 2016. The book endeavors to help both experienced and inexperienced individuals make wise investing decisions.

REFERENCES

1. Keister, L. A. (2003). Religion and Wealth: The Role of Religious Affiliation and Participation in Early Adult Asset Accumulation. *Social Forces,* 82, 173-205.

2. Ibbotson, R., Kaplan, P. (2000). "Does Asset Allocation Policy Explain 40, 90, or 100 Percent of Performance?" *Financial Analysts Journal*, 56(1), 26-33.

3. Rogers, J. (2004). *Hot Commodities: How Anyone Can Invest Profitably in the World's Best Market.* Random House.

4. Conover, C.M., Jensen, G.R., Johnson. E.R., and Mercer., J.M. (2010). Is now the time to add commodities to your portfolio? *J. Invest.*, 19, 10-19.

5. Barrasm, L., Scaillet, O., Wermers, R. (2010). False discoveries in mutual fund performance: Measuring luck in estimated alphas. *Journal of Finance*, 65(1), 179-216.

6. Elton, E., Gruber, M., Brown, S., Goetzmann, W. (2014). *Modern Portfolio Theory and Investment Analysis.* Hoboken, NJ: Wiley & Sons.

7. Rabbi Ari Marburger. *Tzedaka and Maase rKesafim: A Practical Guide to Giving Charity.*

INDEX